Chevrolet History:
1929-1939

By John D. Robertson

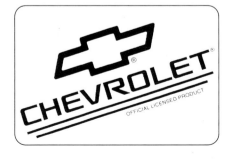

Library of Congress Cataloging-In-Publication Date ISBN 1-880524-25-2

Published by **Cars & Parts Magazine,**
The Voice of the Collector Car Hobby Since 1957

Cars & Parts Magazine is a division of Amos Press Inc.,
911 Vandemark Road, Sidney, Ohio 45365

Also publishers of:
Cars & Parts Collector Car Annual
Catalog of American Car ID Numbers 1950-59
Catalog of American Car ID Numbers 1960-69
Catalog of American Car ID Numbers 1970-79
Catalog of Camaro ID Numbers 1967-93
Catalog of Chevy Truck ID Numbers 1946-72
Catalog of Ford Truck ID Numbers 1946-72
Catalog of Chevelle, Malibu & El Camino ID Numbers 1964-87
Catalog of Pontiac GTO ID Numbers 1964-74
Catalog of Corvette ID Numbers 1953-93
Catalog of Mustang ID Numbers 19641/2-93
Catalog of Thunderbird ID Numbers 1955-93
Catalog of Firebird ID Numbers 1967-93
Catalog of Oldsmobile 4-4-2, W-Machine &
   Hurst/Olds ID Numbers 1964-91
Catalog of Chevy Engine V-8 Casting Numbers 1955-93
Ultimate Collector Car Price Guide
Automobiles of America
Corvette: American Legend (The Beginning)
Corvette: American Legend (1954-55 Production)
The Resurrection of Vicky
Peggy Sue – 1957 Chevrolet Restoration
Suzy Q.: Restoring a '63 Corvette Sting Ray

Dedication

Over the years a number of persons have suffered to some extent as a result of my automotive addiction. They include: my late parents, John Richards Robertson and Geraldine Robertson, whose Detroit neighbors periodically threatened, in the mid-1950s, to get up a petition regarding my raggedy bunch of old cars and the use of certain loud power tools. My brother, Dr. Paul L. Robertson, now residing in Australia, has never owned a Chevy but once got close with a Holden. My children, Mrs. Jeanne Lapinski, Mrs. Jill Hoyle, Mrs. Lynne McClannahan and Miss Julie Robertson, who spent vacations sitting in a hot car while Dad explored junkyards and found themselves marching through mud in Hershey, Pa. when they were supposed to be in school during certain weeks in October. Whose weekends were spent at car shows and swap meets. Who were pressed into involuntary service whenever Dad needed to get a car to the trim shop or drag the latest prize home at the end of a big chain. Yeah, they were and are great kids. Funny thing though, none of them ever even dated car guys. Strange.

Contents

Preface 5

About the Author 6

Introduction 8

1929: The International Series debuts 12

1930: 'Body by Fisher' and more power 30

1931: Worm and sector steering adopted 52

1932: Styling zenith 80

1933: 'Aer-Stream' Styling and no-draft ventilation 100

1934: Knee Action suspension, 80 horsepower
      and 80 miles per hour 126

1935: Showcasing Fisher's unique "Turret Top" 148

1936: Hydraulic brakes and all-steel bodies 172

1937: 'Diamond Crown' styling 195

1938: New grilles, trim; voltage regulator added 220

1939: Vacuum-shift debuts; no open model in the line .. 246

Preface

The General Motors Media Archives located in the heart of Detroit has been called a priceless treasure. For a number of years I had heard rumors of a crowded, evil smelling room in a back corner of GM Photographic somewhere in Detroit's New Center. It was said that the room was almost abandoned (untrue), disorganized (somewhat true), very aromatic (true) and a virtual gold mine of automotive photography (also true). During my years with GM Photographic at the Technical Center in Warren, Mich., I occasionally had reason to visit the New Center location but never saw the mysterious "vinegar room."

Shortly after my transfer to the new Center I was asked to look at some images selected at random and printed from negatives in the "vinegar room." Wow! The rumor was true. Several things were abundantly clear: The variety of makes (predominantly but not exclusively GM), models, and eras was great, the quality of the original photography was generally superb and most of the images had survived very well. As it turned out, the collection had never been abandoned; to the contrary new images were added yearly. The earliest images were more than 100 years old, the newest were of current model vehicles. A staff of skilled and dedicated archivists and preservationists was being assembled to organize this treasure, identify and index the contents, and enter it into a highly sophisticated computer system. Once in the system and on-line, the system would make all photographic images, videos and films in GM available to the divisions and their agencies. "Would you like to help select and identify some images for a capabilities display?" Well sure, I'm always willing to help out! It was then that I was shown the "vinegar room." That's when the idea was born that resulted in this, which is planned as the first in a series of photo books based on the "priceless treasure."

After several years of operation, The Media Archives, now a department of General Motors Communications Support Group, is on target scanning images and refiling them in environmentally friendly surroundings. The collection, possibly the largest of its kind, contains more than three million negative images, more than two thousand reels of film and at least 10,000 video tape masters. You are invited to browse these pages and add a silent word of gratitude to those who have, over the years, had the foresight to preserve this treasure for the enjoyment of future generations.

About the Author

John Robertson and his "first car," a 1938 Chevrolet pedal car.

John D. Robertson is employed in the General Motors Media Archives as a product expert. He was born into a car family: a grandmother wound Model T coils at Ford's Highland Park plant; his father, mother, grandfather and several uncles were Chrysler employees; and while growing up he had relatives working for General Motors, Hudson and Kaiser-Frazer. He claims his first word was "car." At age three, in 1940, he entertained the safety boys at the nearest street corner by identifying the popular makes of cars and even a few model years. The pivotal point in his life was the first Floyd Clymer Scrapbook. *Time* magazine published a review of Clymer's book and seven-year-old John pestered his parents until they found a copy. This book and subsequent Clymer books were read until they were in tatters and patched with Scotch tape for further reading.

When the family moved to the Rosedale Park section of Detroit in 1945, John began to hang around the local Chevrolet dealer, bombarding the salesmen and mechanics with questions and opinions. Within a few years of the end of World War II, there were dealers for all makes within an easy bicycle ride of his home. These were visited on a regular basis. John's first car was a twenty-dollar 1929 Model A Ford acquired at age 14. His first "real" car was a three-year-old 1950 Dodge Wayfarer passed down when the family got a new Plymouth. The Dodge got the then mandatory fender skirts and two inch lowering blocks, but the senior Robertson vetoed a glasspack muffler. John's first Chevrolet was a 1937 Master Deluxe Sport Sedan. His first new Chevrolet was a 1969 Impala, which coincided with his employment at the Jam Handy Organization working as an engineering liaison on the Chevrolet account. His favorite Chevrolet was a turquoise and white 1954 Bel Air that he drove daily while teaching in a one-room school.

John knows how difficult it is to explain that the house payment money was accidentally spent to buy yet another old car. He thinks he's had three hundred, maybe four hundred cars; some never ran, others never got home. John has written articles for Cars & Parts on and off since 1983 and also was an occasional contributor to Corvette News. Over the years John worked on Chevrolet, Chrysler and Toyota accounts at several agencies before joining General Motors. He has four grown daughters and lives with a tolerant redhead, a cat and usually around 10 cars in a house with a six-car garage in Shelby Township, Mich.

Introduction

In 1929 Chevrolet introduced one of the most important cars in automotive history. The 1929 Chevrolet was truly a milestone. It wasn't Chevrolet's first six cylinder, that honor went to the very first Chevrolet, the Classic Six of 1912. It was, however, Chevrolet's first overhead valve six and it was a real bargain. In total sales over the next 26 years the Chevrolet OHV six powered more vehicles than any other engine in the world. It was, in fact, so successful that it powered the world's best selling car in 20 of those 26 years (actually 23 years as the war years of 1943, 1944, 1945 are not included). These early sixes quickly earned a reputation for reliable, economical performance.

There were other popular price sixes in 1929 but it was the Chevrolet that was the six cylinder success story. Other low price sixes that year included Hudson's Essex and Willys' Whippet. The major competitor was Ford's four-cylinder Model A. Another four cylinder, Chrysler's Plymouth launched in 1928, was destined to seriously challenge both Chevrolet and Ford for several decades before eventually yielding market position to GM's medium-priced cars. Generally slightly more expensive, Plymouths were known as engineers' cars and were, indeed, quite innovative in their first few years (some models were also rather stylish as well).

Before 1929 ended Wall street had laid its well known egg and auto sales were on a fast slide down from the year's record-setting pace. Conceived as a better version of every man's car, this new roomy, stylish six-cylinder Chevy was also a very viable consideration for families who wanted to or were forced to move down from Buicks or possibly even Packards or Marmons. While a huge number of working folks were stricken from the rolls of potential Chevrolet buyers for the balance of the depression, these new sixes were to prove quite appealing to those moving out of premium makes.

Chevrolet, unlike Ford, was the product of the best thinking of committees, or work groups, who were very alert to the rising aspirations of car owners. In 1928, during the developmental period of the Chevrolet Six, GM employed more than one thousand engineers. A Ford car, on the other hand, was the automotive incarnation of the personal preferences of one man who had begun, by the mid twenties, to lose touch with the public. General Motors Chairman, Alfred Sloan, realized that the key to success was not going to be found in building duplicate Fords. He reasoned that

people would pay a little more to get a noticeably more upscale product. Chevrolet buyers could even feel somewhat smug about paying a bit more to upgrade themselves out of the Model T into a stylish and colorful car with a real gear shift. It made a statement that could be easily recognized by one's circle of friends and neighbors as well as everyone else on the road. Ford yielded a bit adding some colors and a bright radiator shell but the public had tasted low-cost luxury and they wanted more.

In 1927, Chevrolet's contemporary styling and upscale features had forced Ford to discontinue the Model T. The all-new Model A was introduced near the end of the year. The long changeover shutdown had enabled Chevrolet to capture first place in sales that year. Ford sales rebounded. Chevrolet trumped with the new six in 1929 and Ford went back to the drawing boards, responding with the V-8 in mid-year 1932. The thrifty Depression era consumer wasn't sure that eight-cylinder cars could deliver the economies of operation and maintenance that they craved. Chevrolet's six was frequently perceived as just the right size. It was, the buyers reasoned, smoother than Ford's four and more economical than Ford's V-8. Premium models from Chevrolet such as the Special Sedans of 1930, 1931 and 1932 offered unique luxury touches to buyers in the low-price field. The greater length of the in-line six engine dictated a longer hood than those required for vehicles with four cylinder or V-8 engines. Long hoods were a familiar styling cue of luxury cars and they added greatly to the appeal of the 1931 and 1932 Chevrolets. In addition, the much admired 1932 also incorporated the hood side panel doors which had looked so elegant on the 1931 Cadillacs. This attention to detail and emphasis on quality touches, some small, some quite significant, is evident when Chevrolets of the pre-WW II era are compared to their competitors. The added value brought to the marketplace by GM Art and Color, Fisher Body and even the Ternstedt division combined to make Chevrolets jewel-like in comparison to their competitors. The car buyers of 1931 rewarded Chevrolet with the sales crown and repeated the compliment in most succeeding years.

The Great Depression, as it was known, put the automobile manufacturers in a very real death struggle competing against each other for the favor of the few buyers left in the marketplace. Prices were cut and re-cut to remain competitive. It was progress and innovation, however, that would be the most effective ways to put a vehicle ahead of the competition. Those remaining new car buyers were the real winners in this game of escalating technology and design excellence. The products were getting demonstrably better each year, bristling with features and getting more sophisticated in the areas now known as NVH (noise, vibration and harshness). It was in the 11-year period examined by this book that the automobile evolved into a quiet, smooth, all-season vehicle capable of all-day operation at highway speeds. It was a time in which the manufacturers were able to go from concept to production in a year or less with no federal requirements for mountains of certification documents. The engineers were all engaged in making the product more pleasing, more usable at a reasonable price. An example of this was Fisher No-Draft Ventilation, the most important new feature of the redesigned 1933 models. It was also in 1933 that Chevrolet pioneered a new marketing strategy which treated the low-price field as two separate segments, one willing to pay for nothing more than basic transportation, rather like the old Ford market of a few years earlier. The other, like the original Chevrolet market, was willing to pay a bit more for a nicer car with a more upscale image. To address both of these segments within the low-price market, Chevrolet fielded two distinctly different series, the 107 inch wheelbase Standard and the 110 inch wheelbase Master. The Standard was powered by a slightly smaller 180.9-cid version of the Master's 206.8-cid engine. The strategy was successful and in 1934 the gap between the Standard and the Master series widened as the Master debuted knee-action independent front suspension. This feature also widened the gap between Chevrolet and Ford, which would continue to offer the antiquated transverse front and rear suspension for 14 additional years.

The mid-1930s were also a time of rapid styling changes as everybody tried to figure which of the numerous approaches to streamlining would be best received by the public. 1935 was a year of major change with the arrival of Chevrolet's all-new Master Deluxe series. The Standard series was a near-visual duplicate of its 1934 counterpart. This strategy, which incorporated appeals to both the innovators and the more traditional buyers, should have guaranteed success. It didn't. Ford also had an all new design for 1935 and was able to recapture the sales crown for the first time since 1930. Chevrolet's setback was short-lived. Important engineering and styling refinements in the Master Deluxe series and an all-new design for the Standard returned Chevrolet to first place in sales where it was destined to remain for many years. All 1936 Chevrolets featured hydraulic brakes. Ford would wait three more years before adding this important feature.

By 1937 many Americans (predominantly those who were employed) believed that the Great Depression was over and automobile sales were spirited. Chevrolet sales dropped somewhat compared to those of 1936, but Chevrolet retained the sales crown. The threat was two-pronged; medium-price cars enjoyed a sales surge as did Ford which almost caught Chevrolet. Much Chevrolet production was lost to sit-down strikes early in the model year. Toward the end of the year the economy stalled signaling the recession of 1938. Chevrolet styling was basically carryover in 1938 with a few well done refinements in grille, hood louvers and ornamentation. Ford launched

an ambitious program in 1938 with two distinctly different series, the Standard and the Deluxe. The more streamlined Deluxe didn't find the buyer support that Ford had anticipated. The Standard was a facelift of the 1937 "humpback" model. Almost 60 years later, Ford collectors still tend to bypass the 1938 models while Chevrolet's 1938 offerings continue to please.

While the first of the "stovebolt" Chevrolets, the 1929s, coincided with the start of the Great Depression, the last model treated in this book, 1939, represents the year that probably marked the end of that Depression. Powerful winds of change were sweeping across Europe as Adolf Hitler prepared to throw the world into war. While not actually threatened at the time, the United States began to support England and France with war materiel. This sudden demand on the production and labor resources of America effectively broke the back of the depression and ushered the nation into a war-time economy. On the civilian front, the 1939 cars were good sellers and Chevrolet's new models led the way as buyers again endorsed Chevrolet as America's favorite.

This 1929 Chevrolet four-door sedan is wearing optional front and rear bumpers.

1929: The International Series debuts

The 1929 Chevrolet International Series was a dramatic new vehicle. The most important feature was, of course, the new 194-cid valve-in-head six cylinder engine rated at 46 horsepower, up 11 from the previous year's four cylinder. Chevrolet's near-trademark disc wheels were continued with wire or wood spoke artillery wheels available but decidedly unpopular. Four wheel mechanical brakes were used with those on the rear being the external contracting type while the front employed the now more familiar internal-expanding configuration.

The new Chevrolet had many selling features when contrasted to the primary competitor, the Model A Ford. Among these were a 107-inch wheelbase, 3.5 inches greater than that of the Model A. The frame itself was longer, 150 inches vs. Ford whose partial frame was only 115 inches long. The Chevrolet had seven cubic feet more interior room, greater braking area, gasoline tank located in rear, four springs of chrome vanadium steel vs. two springs, carburetor accelerating pump, motor heat indicator on dash, and oil pressure gauge on dash. While the Model A was sometimes thought of as the "baby Lincoln," the new Chevrolet showed some LaSalle influence.

The contemporary new body featured new belt line and window reveal treatments contributing to a lower look and hood side panels sported fewer louvers, which were now clustered toward the rear of the panels. The new plated radiator shell was taller and narrower and bright headlamp supports were added. A lavish new prestige model was added but discontinued before the end of the year. Known as the Imperial Landau, it was a blind quarter sedan with a folding roof section over the rear seat. The handsome new vehicle was replaced by the Imperial sedan which lacked the Imperial Landau's folding roof but was a near twin in appearance. While there were no really "cheap looking" Chevrolets in 1929, the convertible Landau, Imperial Landau and Sport Cabriolet models were especially well trimmed and could have mixed well in just about any social situation.

This is the rear mounted spare tire carrier and center tail lamp for a 1929 Chevrolet.

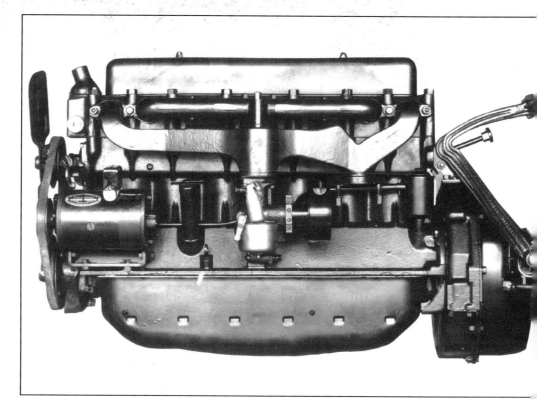

The new 194-cid six-cylinder engine brought new levels of sophistication to the low-price field.

This attractive instrument cluster housed the speedometer and gauges for oil pressure, engine temperature and ammeter.

This 1929 Chevrolet two-door Coach is undergoing testing in the cold room at the GM Research Labs in Detroit. Note the 1929 Michigan manufacturer's license plate.

'29

A 1929 Chevrolet two-door Coach is posed in front of the grid at the Milford Proving Ground for its official front end shot.

Shown in these photos is a 1929 Chevrolet Convertible Landau with top down and top up. The optional bumpers have not been installed on this vehicle.

A 1929 Chevrolet two-door Coach is shot against a garage wall at Milford. This is a completely base version of Chevrolet's most popular body style.

Four lovely young ladies model the latest in Roaring '20s fashions in a 1929 Chevrolet Sport Cabriolet in the auditorium of the General Motors Building in November 1928.

The touring car was rapidly losing favor by the time this 1929 Chevrolet was shot in front of the Chicago Pneumatic Tool Co. facility at 6201 Second Boulevard in Detroit.

We apologize for the heavily retouched 1929 Chevrolet Coupe but couldn't resist showing the company car assigned to Chevrolet's field men that year.

14833-C4

This was the competitive target, the 1929 version of Ford's sales leading Model A.

Hudson's 1929 Essex Coach was the most popular of the competitive lower-priced six-cylinder models. Note the body seam rising from the peak of the rear fender. This allowed sharing some stampings with the four-door models.

A Willys Whippet, one of the other makes competing in the low-price field.

Chrysler's new entry in the low-price field was the Plymouth, a four-cylinder descendant of the Maxwell.

14833-C7

Compare this 1929 DeSoto with the Plymouth. Early DeSotos were, in reality, six-cylinder Plymouths and as such, slightly up-market competition for the new Chevrolet.

In the summer of 1930 Chevrolet sent out a press release showing this 1929 Chevrolet which one Inspector Zerambo (rhymes with Rambo) drove into the whirling propeller of this small plane to capture a pair of smuggled aliens. The damage to the car is unexpectedly light.

This is probably one of the most elegant Chevrolets of all time, the 1929 Convertible Landau with folding rear quarter.

We try to avoid heavily retouched photos but this was the only 1929 Imperial Sedan we could find. This model replaced the exotic Convertible Landau in mid-year.

1930: 'Body by Fisher' and more power

The 1930 Chevrolets were very close relatives of their 1929 predecessors. The mechanical refinements included a switch to internal expanding for the rear brakes, a bump in horsepower from 46 to 50, new hydraulic shock absorbers and a change from 20 inch to 19 inch wheels. Those wheels were more likely to be wire wheels this year as they were standard equipment on the Sport Roadster, Sport Coupe and Special Sedan. The hubcaps for these wire wheels were noticeably larger than those used with the 1929 wire wheels. Disc wheels were standard on all other models with wire wheels optional. Wood spoke wheels were again available.

The sedan lineup was revised this year with the new Special Sedan at the top of the line. The Special Sedan was well equipped with interior luxury touches, cowl lights and sidemounts to appeal to those moving down from higher-priced makes. The Sedan was upgraded with chrome plated cowl lights and a chrome plated cowl molding. The lowest-priced sedan was the Club Sedan, a stripped version of the premium Landau Sedan of 1929. The Club Sedan could be tricked out with optional wire wheels and landau bars for a look of formal elegance. The Cabriolet of 1929 was discontinued for 1930. The instrument panel was modified this year with the discontinuance of the previous instrument cluster. All gauges were now positioned in separate cutouts in the dash panel.

Composite body by Fisher continued to be a very important difference between Chevrolet and Ford. Chevrolet pointed out that the "highest priced cars all use the combination of hardwood-and-steel construction because it is the finest and the best." The Fisher VV windshield was another talking point. Unlike the hinged wing nut type of folding windshields, the Chevrolet windshield could be cranked open or closed with just one hand. Ford's new styling for 1930 followed Chevrolet's cues of 1929 with a taller, narrower radiator hood and cowl as well as smaller wheels. As the Model A lost its rounded look and became more angular it also looked less like a Lincoln.

This 1930 Chevrolet two-door Coach is equipped with an auxiliary bottle to supply a measured quart of fuel. Compare the angle of the windshield with that of the 1929 two-door Coach.

The young lady is turning the crank that raises the windshield for maximum ventilation. This view also shows Chevrolet's new instrument configuration for 1930.

A 1930 Chevrolet chassis displays a drum for the new internal expanding rear brakes.

This is the well appointed interior of a 1930
Chevrolet Special Sedan.

This close-up on a 1930 Chevrolet Special Sedan
reveals a wealth of details, including the very
impressive radiator cap, cowl lamp, honeycomb
radiator and more.

A pretty little 1930 Chevrolet Sport Coupe shows off the new wire wheels. The handsome fire station is still serving Detroit's new center area.

This pair of 1930 Chevrolet Sedan Deliveries is ready for delivery to the R.H. Fyfe and Co. The location is across Milwaukee Ave. from the old Chevrolet Central Office.

This Ft. Wayne Indiana family owned five new Chevrolet sixes in 1930. Note the aftermarket headlight visors.

The factory approved spot-light is shown on a 1930 Chevrolet Sport Coupe.

Hard to believe today but this traffic-stopping crowd gathered in front of Flint, Michigan's Summerfield Chevrolet on May 30, 1930 to view the drawing for a new Chevrolet.

This scene in the General Motors Building showroom of the Chevrolet Retail Store shows a threesome of 1930 Chevrolets: a two-door Coach with optional wheels, a Club Sedan with wire wheels and a Sedan with disc wheels.

This 1930 Chevrolet Special Sedan displays wire wheels, side-mounts and luggage rack.

A 1930 Chevrolet two-passenger Coupe shot on the roof of the General Motors Research Building. It has optional wire wheels and bumpers. When wire wheels were supplied the tail light moved from the spare tire carrier to the left frame rail.

With the hood open, a salesman shows off the six-cylinder engine of an elegant 1930 Chevrolet Club Sedan.

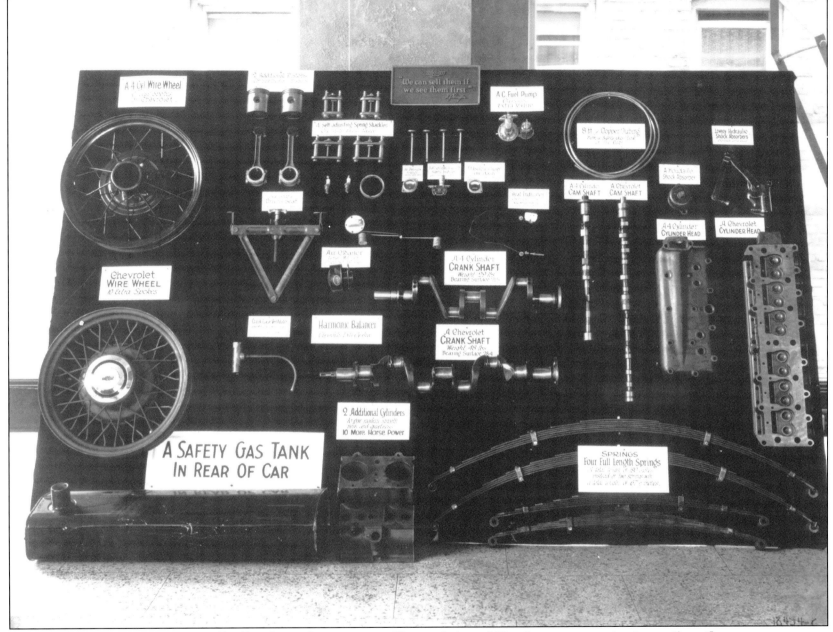

This tear-down component display board contrasts Chevrolet and Ford components, targeting the areas of Chevrolet superiority.

Apparently a prototype or perhaps a full-scale model, this 1930 Chevrolet Sport Roadster is supported on blocks.

No, the 1930 Chevrolet Phaeton is not parked in a fog bank, an artist has "blown out" the background to highlight the vehicle.

The 1930 Chevrolet two-passenger Roadster wore standard disc wheels. It is shown here with the top up.

This current model 1930 Chevrolet two-door Coach is being subjected to some sort of brake test. The technician is using a remote unit connected to a Bean machine.

A Chevrolet salesman explains the service policy while delivering a new 1930 four-door sedan in the shop area.

The headlamp of a 1930 Chevrolet as seen from the rear. The rim was bright, the bucket painted on most vehicles. This chrome bucket was filmed on an export phaeton.

This is the factory side curtain treatment for a 1930 Chevrolet Phaeton.

Here's an unusual angle on a 1930 Chevrolet Phaeton showing ample rear seat leg room.

We have no explanation to offer on the low placement of the cowl light on this 1930 Chevrolet Phaeton, except that the file was marked "export."

A nice underhood shot showing the left side of a 1930 Chevrolet engine as it left the factory.

1931:
Worm and sector steering adopted

The 1931 Chevrolets, advertised as "The Great American Value," featured attractive new bodies accented by stylish belt moldings and window shapes. The headlamps were now chromed and rode on a chrome bar. Gone were the headlamp stands of 1929 and 1930. Hood louvers extended most of the length of the hood side panel. Two new bumper designs were used during the year. A modified version of the two-bar design gave way to a wider, more curved one-bar design in interim 1931. If the new Chevrolets looked bigger it was no accident. Wheelbases had increased by two inches from 107 to 109 inches. The 194-cid engine continued to turn out 50 horsepower. Engine improvements included a more rigid crankshaft and a more efficient harmonic balancer. The new, worm and sector steering gear resulted in reduced steering effort.

The handsome blind quartered Club sedan of 1930 was discontinued while several new body styles were introduced. The five-passenger coupe arrived to challenge Ford's Victoria. A convertible version of the five-passenger coupe was known as the Landau Phaeton. Unlike the Ford A-400 whose upper window frames remained in place when the top and windows were lowered, the Landau Phaeton was wide open when the top and windows were lowered. It was actually the forerunner of the convertible coupes of the 1940s.

Promotion of the Fisher composite body continued with the most glowing description to date; "This is not only the strongest, safest, most durable type known, but it is exactly the same type used in the highest-priced cars. A framework of selected hardwood is fortified at all points of stress by staunch steel bracing. Over this strong framework are mounted sturdy steel panels, so that the wood reinforces the steel and the steel reinforces the wood."

1931 was a depression year and a bad one. In a comparative sense, however, it was a good year for Chevrolet which outsold Ford and every other maker to regain the sales crown. It is not surprising that the Model A in its fourth year ran out of steam. Chevrolet had topped Ford with the six in 1929 and delivered a heavy blow with very attractive new styling in 1931. Meanwhile, with the exception of a painted fill on the upper radiator shell and a slanted windshield post on some models, the 1931 Fords looked like warmed-over 1930s. Over in Highland Park, Plymouth launched the lower PA with floating power, which nearly eliminated the vibration that characterized four-cylinder engines. This innovation was a severe competitive challenge to

Ford whose Model A was still a four. The effect on Chevrolet sales was probably negligible. In fact, Chevrolet's return to sales leadership may have been helped by Plymouth's conquest sales to former Ford intenders.

The new Independence AE Series of 1931 underwent several key changes, including a wheelbase lengthened by two inches and the addition of chromed headlight rims and taillight housings, Lovejoy hydraulic shock absorbers, and fully enclosed four-wheel mechanical brakes. In addition, wire wheels became standard. Several new body styles debuted, but this four-door sedan wasn't one of them. New for '31 were a Cabriolet, a Landau Phaeton and a five-passenger Coupe.

A 1931 Chevrolet Phaeton with top raised. The cowl lights were standard on this model.

This 1931 Chevrolet two-passenger Roadster is apparently a prototype with a clay body. Note wood slats in the rear wheel well.

A 1931 Chevrolet Sport Roadster was shot in a garage with a sheet obscuring the background. An artist would then "strip" the car on a background with an uphill road.

This 1931 Chevrolet Coach was shot in January 1932 for a used car merchandising program.

The premium closed car in Chevrolet's 1931 line was this Special Sedan. The dual sidemounts were standard on this model.

This is the rear view of a 1931 Chevrolet Landau Phaeton. The spare tire cover would fit better if it had been properly installed.

The 1931 Chevrolet Landau Phaeton is not often seen with the top up and windows rolled down. That massive electrical hookup on the floor feeds the flood lights that lit this shot.

The 1931 Chevrolet Landau Phaeton top folded into a neat bundle and was covered by a nicely tailored boot.

19549-10

This straight front view of a 1931 Chevrolet Landau Phaeton shows the interesting horn design and Goodyear diamond-tread tires.

A 1931 Chevrolet Sport Coupe with occupied rumble seat shows the one piece bumper face bar found on some 1931s.

Here's a 1931 Chevrolet five-passenger Coupe, the stylish response to Ford's Victoria.

The two bar bumper design is seen on this 1931 Chevrolet three-window, two-passenger Coupe.

A 1931 Chevrolet five-window, two-passenger Coupe pauses on a Detroit street. Note the unusual awning design on the home in the background.

The 1931 Chevrolet Cabriolet featured large, functional landau bars for an elegant big car look. The rumble seat was standard.

This angle shows the unique rear-end styling of the new 1931 Chevrolet five-passenger Coupe. A small luggage compartment was featured.

This interior shot of a 1931 Chevrolet two-door Coach clearly shows bucket seat and windlace detail as well as the bow tie front floor mat with Fisher Body emblem centered just ahead of the seats.

Here's the driver's compartment of a 1931 Chevrolet four-door Sedan. The instrument cluster and three-spoke wheel were new.

A 1931 Chevrolet four-door Sedan shows off the new belt and window reveal moldings. This was the last year for that visor.

The rear of a 1931
Chevrolet with
two-bar bumper.

A 1931 Chevrolet Sport Roadster is at its sportiest with the top down and windshield folded. The four college men are well bundled but those hats are history once the car gets rolling.

This 1931 Chevrolet two-door Coach posed in the elegant auditorium of Detroit's General Motors Building in October of 1930. Note the Fisher Body emblem on the carpet.

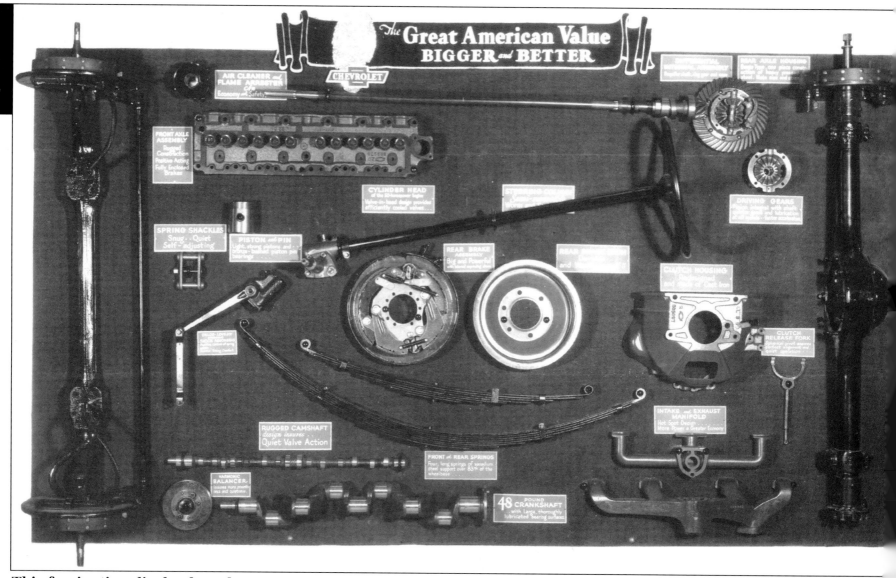

The Great American Value
BIGGER and BETTER

CHEVROLET

AIR CLEANER and FLAME ARRESTER
Economy and Safety

FRONT AXLE ASSEMBLY

CYLINDER HEAD

DRIVING GEARS

SPRING SHACKLES
Snug - Quiet
Self - adjusting

PISTON and PIN

REAR BRAKE ASSEMBLY
Big and Powerful

CLUTCH HOUSING

CLUTCH RELEASE FORK

RUGGED CAMSHAFT
design insures
Quiet Valve Action

INTAKE and EXHAUST MANIFOLD

HARMONIC BALANCER

FRONT and REAR SPRINGS

48 POUND CRANKSHAFT

This fascinating display board was constructed for Chevrolet's 1931 auto show displays. It covers most of the basics from axle to axle.

An accessories display at a Chevrolet dealership in 1931 showed sidemount mirror, radiator stone shield, heater, clock, spotlight, cowl light, single face bar bumpers and more.

A 1931 Chevrolet Sedan Delivery shot on the roof of the General Motors Research Building. The newly standard wire wheels give this business vehicle an almost jaunty appearance.

The rarely seen wooden wheel option is "demonstrated" on a 1931 Chevrolet four-door Sedan. That's the General Motors Building in the background.

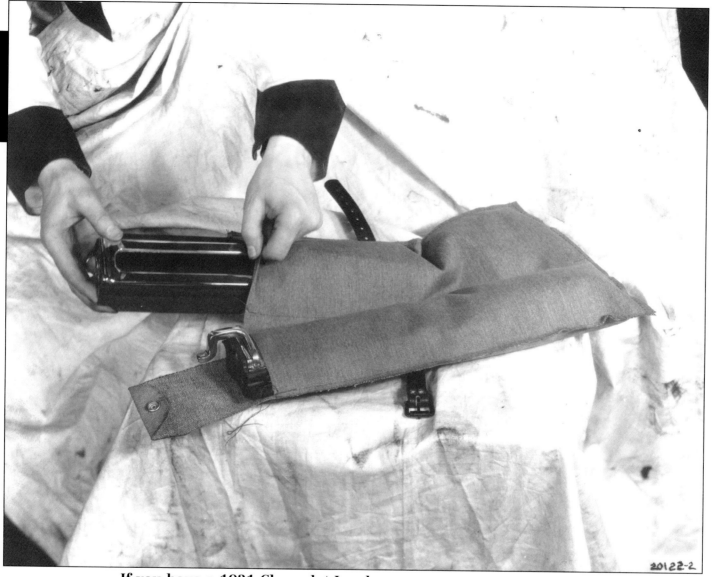

If you have a 1931 Chevrolet Landau Phaeton, you should be storing your removable B posts in a cloth sack like this one.

(At right) The showroom of Johnson Chevrolet in Ferndale, Mich. was typical of the better dealerships of the era with a balcony for viewing the vehicles at one of their most flattering angles.

1932: Styling zenith

If ever there was a car that "clicked" it was the 1932 Chevrolet Confederate Series. A new driver's side adjustable internal sun visor replaced the external cadet type visor. The engine was now rated at 60 horsepower and featured a new Carter downdraft carburetor topped off by a large air cleaner with flame arrestor. A speed of 65 to 70 miles per hour was claimed. The new synchromesh transmission was said to permit "even the inexperienced driver to shift gears easily and noiselessly at all speeds. While using the same basic body as that of the 1931 Independence Series, the 1932 was instantly recognizable for its headlamps. It looked like a 7/8 scale 1931 Cadillac. In a year of generally excellent design the 1932 Chevrolet was a standout.

Chevrolet historians don't seem to be able to reach agreement on what constitutes a Deluxe model 1932. One thing seems certain: at announcement time all Deluxes had chrome hood-side doors. (Chevrolet called them "ports".) Standard cars had painted doors with chrome handles. Deluxes also had cowl lamps which didn't appear on standard models. Early ordering information indicated that, of the 20 models initially offered in 1932, six were Standards, nine were Deluxes with standard dual sidemounts. The balance, a series of five models, were called neither Deluxe nor Standard. Those vehicles were factory equipped with chrome hood ports and cowl lights. They were identical to the Deluxe models except that they did not have sidemounts.

Merchandising materials effective April 1, 1932 listed 14 models — all with sidemounts available optionally at a cost of $15. The two tires and tubes were extra cost. An engineering release dated March 25, 1932 indicated that the sidemounts were still standard equipment on Special Sedans. With the exception of certain interior trim items, there was no hard and fast rule as to what constituted a Deluxe model. There were, in fact, only two designated as such by April 1, the Deluxe Coupe and the Deluxe Coach. The Convertible Cabriolet, five-passenger Coupe, Landau Phaeton and Standard Coupe (three-window) all carried chrome hood ports and cowl lights but not the Deluxe name. Sport models were rumble seat models of the roadster and five-window coupe with chrome hood ports and cowl lights. The balance of the line, Roadster, Standard five-window Coupe, Coach, Phaeton (touring) and Standard Sedan, carried painted

Many historians and collectors consider the '32 model the most glamorous of all pre-war Chevys. The Confederate Series BA included Standard and Deluxe lines. One of the major differences was that Deluxe models had their hood ports chromed; which makes this two-passenger coupe a Standard issue. Production that year dipped to 323,100, down almost half from 1931. The drop was attributed in part to the continuing Great Depression, but a more likely culprit was the hot selling new V-8 Ford.

hood ports and no cowl lights. Over the years restorers who have added chrome hood ports and/or cowl lights to cars not originally so equipped have helped to further obscure the issue. We believe that the dealers were also happy to add chrome hood ports and cowl lights to lesser cars if that's what it took to make a sale.

Having regained the sales crown in 1931, Chevrolet was dealing from a position of strength in 1932. Ford was not, of course, going to give up easily. The desire to continue the Model A must have been very strong but the will to win dictated that Ford field a competitive product in a period of spiraling technology. The initial series of 1932 Fords, the Model B, featured

lower bodies and fresh new styling set off by a painted radiator shell with a separate grille insert. In late March the Model B was joined by the V-8. While the 1932 models were attractive and more refined than the Model A, they still didn't look like big cars. For one thing the hood was still stubby and the 106-inch wheelbase was shorter by three inches than that of Chevrolet. While there can be no doubt that the V-8 scored big with younger drivers, 1932 was the bottom of the depression and few of those young drivers were qualified buyers. Chevrolet's appeal was greater to the folks who had some money and Chevrolet celebrated another year of sales superiority.

A 1932 Chevrolet Cabriolet showing the rear window shape. If this were an early Deluxe it would have dual sidemounts.

A 1932 Chevrolet Sport Coupe. The "Sport" designated a rumble seat model.

(At left)
This was the announcement
day of the 1932 models at the
Chevrolet Retail Store in the
General Motors Building in
Detroit.

A 1932 Chevrolet five-passenger Coupe. The chrome bullet-shaped headlights were new this year.

The painted hood ports and absence of cowl lights tell us that this is a 1932 Chevrolet Standard five-window, two-passenger Coupe (later called a five-window Coupe).

Staff members of Gainesville Chevrolet in Florida pose with a 1932 Special Sedan. Gas was pumped at the curb.

This 1932 Chevrolet Cabriolet has an optional spotlight and rare metal spare tire cover.

A 1932 Chevrolet Special Sedan is being serviced at Mid City Chevrolet in Chicago. It is loaded with accessories including trunk rack and trunk, metal sidemount covers, spotlight, wind deflectors and stainless spoke covers.

Central Chevrolet in Philadelphia had this large showroom in 1932. A cut-away transmission is mounted on the display at the left.

A 1932 Chevrolet Deluxe Landau Phaeton with trunk rack and sidemount mirror is on display in the Chevrolet Retail Store showroom in Detroit's General Motors Building. In April the Deluxe name disappeared on this model and the sidemounts became an option.

If this 1932 Chevrolet Landau Phaeton were an early Deluxe model it would have dual sidemounts. Actually, the rear-mounted spare adds the illusion of greater length.

A full frontal view of a 1932 Chevrolet Landau Phaeton shows the standard single trumpet horn.

This rear view of a 1932 Chevrolet Standard Roadster shows the interesting sculpturing treatment on the rear quarter panel above the fenders.

This is the 1932 Chevrolet Standard Roadster. Even in Standard form the roadster was a standout.

This is the smoking set in the front compartment of a 1932 Chevrolet Special Sedan. The "eye" in the center of the lighter glowed when ready for use.

This view of the windshield header of a 1932 Chevrolet Special Sedan shows the winder knob used to raise or lower the windshield, optional clock mirror, wind deflectors and spotlight handle.

Twin trumpet horns are shown on this 1932 Chevrolet Special Sedan as well as detail of the accessory side mount mirror.

THIS CAR DRIVEN
OVER 106,000 MILES
IN 11 MOS. BY CHAS. LARKIN
Original PISTONS RINGS
PINS BRAKES

NALL & CO.
IOWA CITY, IOWA

OFFICE

25733·18

Shot in 1933, this 1932 Chevrolet Special Sedan was apparently a good investment for the original Iowa City owner, who must have spent a lot of time in his car covering 106,000 miles in 11 months.

In a year of exceptional looking product it is perhaps unexpected that one of the most attractive vehicles was the Sedan Delivery. This vehicle has many deluxe features, including the carriage lamps.

1933: 'Aer-Stream' Styling and no-draft ventilation

The era of streamlining came to Chevrolet in 1933 in the form of "Aer-Stream" styling. Following the memorable act of the breathtaking 1932 model was a tall order. The new Master or Eagle series (commonly called Deluxe) and its mid-year companion, the Standard or Mercury series, were up to the task. The public had been quite impressed by the 1932 Graham's skirted fenders and there was a Detroit-wide rush to jump on that bandwagon. The 1933 Chevrolet's new skirted fenders and separate veed radiator grille complemented the stylish body on a new 110-inch wheelbase. Closed cars featured Fisher no-draft ventilation employing vent windows in front doors and in the quarter windows of the four-door sedan. Plunger-type door lock buttons were added for convenience and security. The five-passenger coupe of 1931 and 1932 was redesigned with a built-in trunk and renamed the Town Sedan. The Landau Phaeton was discontinued. The Starterator combined the starter and accelerator in one functional pedal to "end hard starting, fumbling and stalling." The new octane selector was a simple device which would allow one to set the spark advance for the octane rating of available gasoline. This was the second year of Free Wheeling which allowed clutch-less shifting.

The new Mercury series reverted to the 107-inch wheelbase last seen in 1930. The Mercury was available in coach, two-passenger coupe and rumble seat couple models. Although the bulk of Mercury sales was probably to fleet or municipal (police) users, the cars were unexpectedly attractive and sporty. While the Eagle series vehicles featured three doors in each hood side panel, the Mercury series vehicles sported a row of bold louvers. Thrifty Depression-era buyers apparently considered the larger Eagle to be a better buy as the more costly vehicles accounted for almost 93 percent of Chevrolet's 1933 sales.

Assembly line workers lower a four-door sedan body onto a 1933 Chevrolet Eagle Series chassis. The restyled line for '33 was a success, pushing production back up beyond the 600,000 mark, roughly double the output of 1932. A fresh design, coupled with a more powerful 65-horse six, proved a strong combination. The wheelbase was also stretched in 1933, one extra inch to 110 inches.

Having won the sales race in 1931 and 1932, Chevrolet was anxious to go for three in a row. Ford was not about to go down without a fight and launched a pair of new vehicles, the four-cylinder Model C and the V-8 Model 40, differing very little in appearance. These well styled, bigger looking vehicles were now on a 112-inch wheelbase. In retrospect it would appear that these big, well styled new Fords should have been a more serious challenge to Chevrolet than they actually were.

1933 was the year that Plymouth launched a six, laid an egg, and made a pretty remarkable recovery. For some unremembered reason Plymouth went from a wheelbase of 112 inches on the 1932 four-cylinder car to 107 inches on the 1933 six-cylinder PC model. The public was underwhelmed. After a crash program and a raid of Dodge's parts bins, Plymouth came out in mid-year with the PD on a 112-inch wheelbase and sales finally took off. When the sales were tabulated Chevrolet was again the winner.

New for 1933 was this Master Town Sedan with integral trunk. This angle shows the close-coupled passenger compartment.

This
interesting
angle of a
Town Sedan
shows the
coordination
of rear
window and
instrument
cluster
shaping.

The number of hood ports was reduced from four to three in 1933. They duplicated the rakish new angle of the radiator grill. This is a Town Sedan.

New to Chevrolet in 1933 was Fisher no-draft Ventilation which could bring in fresh air without blasting occupants.

This is the new 181-cid version of the six-cylinder engine used in the 1933 Chevrolet Standard (Mercury) models.

(At left)
A number of
Detroit's
finest pose
with their
new 1933
Chevrolet
Standard
police cars.

A 1933 Chevrolet Master Sport Coupe with dual trumpet horns.

While not as stylish as the new Town Sedan, this 1933 Chevrolet Master two-door Coach with sidemounts and add-on trunk offered more rear leg room and probably more storage space as well.

This 1933 Chevrolet Master Sport Coupe is wearing the optional metal tire cover. The wheels appear to be chromed.

This 1933 Chevrolet Master four-door Sedan has an optional spotlight and metal spare tire cover.

A 1933 Chevrolet Standard two-door Coach poses with two tall Detroit police officers. Note the high mounted right side spotlight.

The Sporty 1933 Chevrolet Standard Coupe with rumble seat. This was the only year the Standard would offer a rumble seat.

The 1933 Chevrolet Standard two-door Coach. Note prominent hood louvers and painted headlamps with bright rims. This photo was retouched from a Master shown elsewhere in this section and may not portray the correct wheelbase.

Sidemounts with metal covers go very well with the 1933 Chevrolet Master four-door Sedan. Note the separate pivoting vent within the rear quarter window.

This 1933 Chevrolet Master four-door Sedan is shown with trunk rack and rear bumper guards. Sidemounts were sold in pairs in 1933 leading us to wonder where this car's spare tire was.

The five-wheel 1933 Chevrolet Master Coach is shown as most were equipped.

This 1933 Chevrolet Master Coach has been dressed up with trunk rack, sidemounts and metal tire covers.

The well appointed rear compartment of a 1933 Chevrolet Master four-door Sedan shows the rear quarter window portion of the no-draft ventilation. Also visible is the rear window shade, assist strap, robe rail and storage pocket.

A tight shot on the 1933 Chevrolet Master showing the new grille, crank hole cover, headlamps and chromed trumpet horn. Note that the tie bar is now two-piece, connecting the fenders to the radiator shell.

XZ3628-239

X23628-257

This is the front compartment of a 1933 Chevrolet Master with the attractive new instrument cluster.

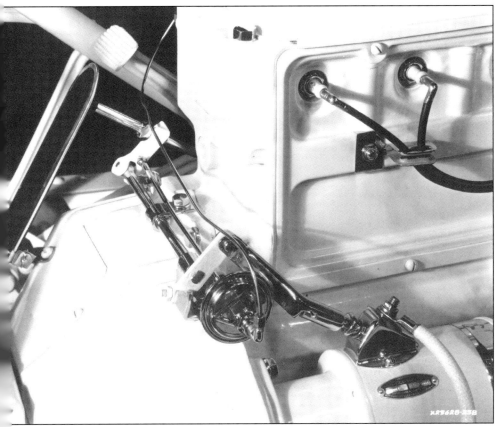

The Starterator was new for 1933 Chevrolet Masters, combining accelerator and starter pedal as one functional unit.

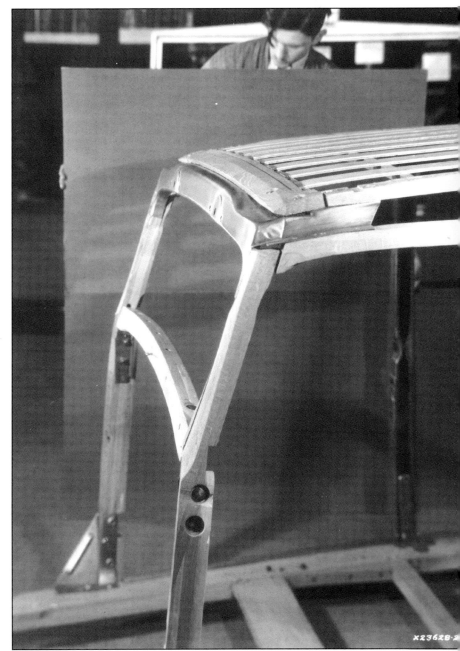

This is the windshield and cowl area of a 1933 Chevrolet composite body showing how wood and steel were combined in the body.

A typical small Chevrolet store of 1933 displays some nice gas pumps.

This is the showroom of Nall Chevrolet during opening week in 1933. A Master four-door Sedan was displayed.

(At left) A 1933 Chevrolet Master Sport Roadster with dual sidemounts and metal tire cover is being serviced in a modern Chicago dealership.

This is the new, bigger 1933 Ford V-8 Tudor shot on a Detroit street. The 110-inch wheelbase helped overcome the stubby look of 1932 Fords.

1934: Knee Action suspension, 80 horsepower and 80 miles per hour

The 1934 Master Chevrolets were the first to feature independent front suspension. Knee-action, as it was known, was a highly significant refinement resulting in riding qualities here-to-fore unknown in low-priced cars. And those cars would perform as well as they rode with the improved Blue-Flame engine, which now turned out 80 horsepower. The new frame was said to be 15 times stronger than frames of conventional design. New front sheet metal construction which Chevrolet called "stabilized," tied all components together as a solid unit to eliminate hood and radiator shake on rough roads.

The streamlining that had begun in 1933 was carried still further in 1934 with more pronounced fender skirting and a more prominent rearward slant to the radiator grille. The previous hood ports were replaced by three horizontal louvers highlighted with bright moldings. A new model, the Sport Sedan, featured an integral trunk and was the four-door equivalent of the Town Sedan. The instruments were now grouped in front of the driver and a lockable glove compartment was added.

Standard models retained the solid front axle, 107-inch wheelbase and 60-horsepower engine of 1933. The Standard series was expanded to include a four-door Sedan, Roadster and Phaeton (touring). The Standard rumble seat coupe was discontinued. The new Standard series accounted for about 17 percent of total 1934 sales.

Modest refinement is the best way to characterize Ford's product program for 1934. Modifications to the grille shell, hood, hubcaps, ornamentation and instrument panel combined with a

With a re-engineered in-line six pumping out a bonus 15 hp, Chevrolet advertised its 1934 line as "80 mph from 80 hp." This sexy Master Roadster carried the new 80-hp Blue Flame engine, while models in the Standard Series retained the old 65-hp engine. Master models also rode on a five-inch longer wheelbase of 112 inches, while Standard versions used a 107-inch wheelbase.

number of mechanical refinements resulting in a rather minor but worthwhile facelift. The unpopular four-cylinder model was dropped mid-year leaving the V-8 as Ford's only engine. Plymouth fielded four lines, three on a 108-inch wheelbase and a new Deluxe on a 114-inch wheelbase. The Deluxe and one of the smaller cars featured independent front suspension. For the second year in a row Plymouth topped its own sales record. In addition to the independent front suspension, Plymouth also featured front vent windows on Deluxe models only. When it was all over, Chevrolet was still in possession of the sales crown.

A soapbox derby racer and a 1934 Chevrolet Sport Sedan. The sport sedan was Chevrolet's first four-door with an integral trunk. Note that the smaller quarter window did not get the Fisher no-draft vent wing found on other Master four-door models. This car has authentic fender shields (skirts).

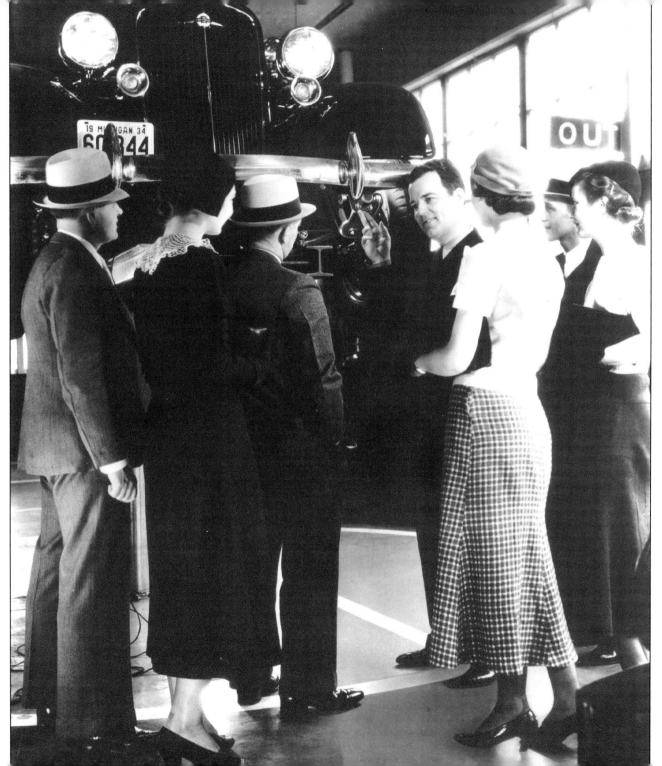

This 1934 Chevrolet Master has been raised to display the new Knee-Action. It is equipped with twin trumpet horns.

129

The 1934 Chevrolet Standard two-door Coach had a roomy interior and front bucket seats.

A 1934 Chevrolet Master Town Sedan was displayed on a pedestal in front of Detroit's GM Building.

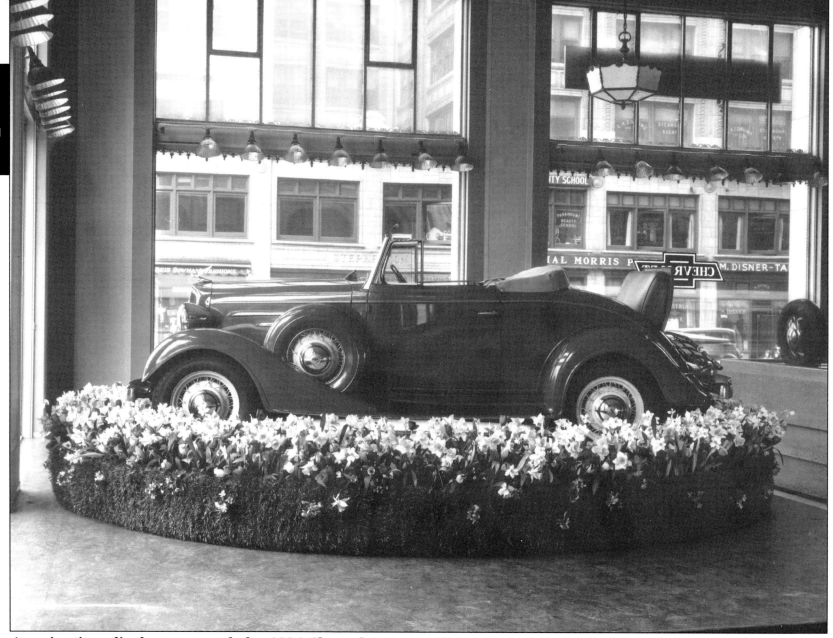

A springtime display surrounded a 1934 Chevrolet Master Cabriolet in the GM Building showroom of Chevrolet's Detroit Retail Store.

A 1934 Chevrolet Standard Six two-door Coach with a metal tire cover and hood ornament is shown on a pedestal in front of the General Motors Building.

This 1934 Chevrolet Master Sport Coupe was on display on West Grand Boulevard in front of the GM Building in April 1934.

The Burlington Zephyr was the last word in rail travel when it was pulled by this Master four-door Sedan in 1934. That chain looks rather puny.

A father and son duo from California has just picked up a pair of 1934 Chevrolet Master four-door Sedans in Detroit. Both are sidemount equipped and the father's car has twin trumpet horns as well.

The modern assembly line was part of the General Motors exhibit at the 1933 and 1934 Chicago World's Fair. Master four-door Sedans and two-door Coaches were assembled. The line on the left is assembling Fisher composite bodies.

27817-2

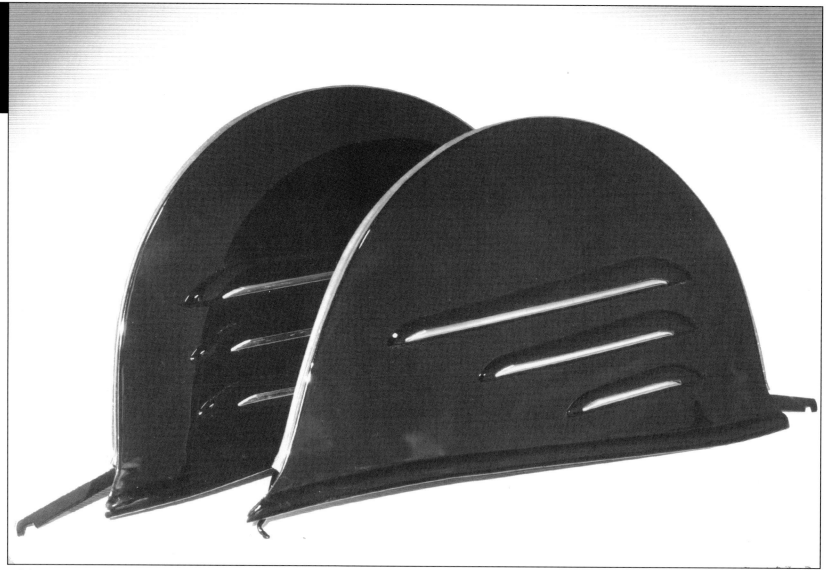

This is a set of 1934 Chevrolet wheel shields. Notice that the louvers replicate those on the hood.

This 1934 Chevrolet Master two-door Coach is really loaded with genuine Chevrolet accessories, including the jeweled headlight visors and fender markers to help drivers avoid garage door jambs.

MOTOR ANALYZING
QUICK SERVICE

Spark
Plugs
CLEANED
AND
ADJUSTED
5¢ EAC.
WHILE
YOU WAIT

WE PREPARE
FOR WIN...NG

CAR

A 1934 Chevrolet Master Sport Sedan is hooked to a motor analyzer while the technician explains the reading to the customer.

Customers rest in comfort surrounded by new 1934 Chevrolets in the showroom of Sight Chevrolet in Kansas.

A well dressed 1934 Chevrolet Master four-door Sedan is parked in front of an accessory display to generate sales.

The rear compartment of a 1934 Chevrolet four-door Sedan offered such comfort and convenience features as a built-in ash receiver, robe rail, foot rest, arm rests and assist straps.

This rear view of a 1934 Chevrolet Master four-door Sedan shows off the larger hubcap unique to the Master models this year.

The Detroit automobile manufacturers frequently donated "safety cars" to the Detroit Police for educational visits to schools. This shot documents the presentation of a new 1934 Chevrolet Master two-door Coach.

Showing a portion of the Chevrolet exhibit at the 1934 New York Auto Show, this shot also included some Oldsmobiles toward the rear.

A 1934 Chevrolet Master Sport Coupe was part of a display at the General Motors Proving Ground in Milford, Michigan in December 1933.

This is a 1934 Chevrolet Master two-passenger Coupe. The improved 80-horsepower engine was said to be good for 80 miles per hour.

The September 1934 display in the lobby of Detroit's GM Building was based on the similarity of Chevrolet's engineering features and those of airplanes.

1935: Showcasing Fisher's unique 'Turret Top'

1935 was a year of maximum and minimum change at Chevrolet dealerships. In the maximum column was the all-new Master Deluxe now riding on a 113-inch wheelbase. The new body sported a low Veed windshield and front doors hinged at the rear to make it easier to swing out of the car. Large semi-teardrop shaped fenders and a sharply angled grille were testimony to Chevrolet's continuing move to streamlining. The most important advance to be found in this new Master Deluxe was the Fisher Turret Top. This type of all-steel seamless roof panel would, within a few years, replace the fabric top insert on closed cars throughout the industry.

Although the Master Deluxe series boasted no open models, sleek three and five window coupes provided a sporty touch in a line dominated by sedans with and without integral trunks. Master Deluxe buyers could now choose a solid axle if Knee-Action wasn't compatible with their needs.

In sharp contrast, the Standard models were near-direct carryovers from 1934. While nicely trimmed and well proportioned, they couldn't compare to their Master Deluxe brothers in terms of contemporary design. Contemporary design was apparently second to cost in the minds of many 1935 car buyers as the Standards rose to 37 percent of Chevrolet sales with Chevrolet's highest volume car being the Standard Coach.

The competition was active in 1935. Plymouth returned to a single series with Standard (Business) and Deluxe models. In some respects Plymouth actually went back a few notches as front vent wings and independent front suspension were no longer available. Many felt that the 1934 Plymouths were more impressive visually than their 1935 successors. Ford's new models could be had with integral trunks but unlike Chevrolet and Plymouth trunk models, the spare was externally mounted at the rear. Ford owners were forced to lift luggage or cargo over the spare to use the trunk. The 1935 Ford also had a shorter hood than the 1934 models but the buyers, if they noticed, seemed to approve. Ford regained the sales crown that year, albeit temporarily.

If this 1935 Chevrolet Master Deluxe looks a bit long, it should. It's a long wheelbase export model. This vehicle may have been derived from taxi components.

This is a 1935 Chevrolet Master Deluxe two-passenger Coupe. The man at the right is a stagehand lighting the shot.

The spare tire lived under a shelf in the spacious trunk of the 1935 Master Deluxe Sport Sedan.

35

The spare tire was still outside on 1935 Chevrolet Master Deluxe Coupes. This five-window Coupe is a two-passenger, non-rumble seat model.

Although integral trunks were gaining popularity, Chevrolet still offered the regular sedan and coach in the 1935 Master Deluxe series with the rear mounted outside spare tire.

The taillight was attached to the trunk lid on 1935 Chevrolet Master Deluxe Sport Sedan and Town Sedan models, which also featured dual trunk handles.

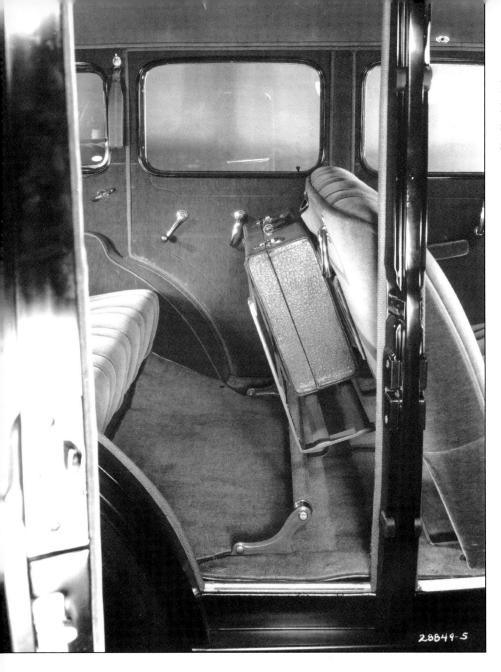

Here is a very seldom seen Chevrolet accessory. The rack attached to the floor of four-door sedans and held suitcases. It was intended for 1935 Standards but is shown on a 1934 Master.

This big visor vanity mirror was available for 1935 Chevrolet Master Deluxes.

This is what you want to look for if you need a bumper jack for a 1935 Chevrolet Master Deluxe.

A full front view of a 1935 Chevrolet Master Deluxe Sport Sedan. The license plate placard incorrectly calls it a trunk sedan.

This display at a Chevrolet salesmen's meeting promotes the clocks available for 1935 Chevrolets along with some antique timepieces.

AT THE END OF THE RAINBOW LIES A POT OF GOLD.

1935 Matched Catalin Accessories

WHEEL SHIELDS

These accessories for 1935 Chevrolets are on display at a salesmen's meeting. Spare tire covers, wheel discs for wire wheels, fender shields (skirts) and more are shown.

Chevrolet actually merchandised this trailer in 1935. Called the "One Wheel Knee-Action Trailer," it looks pretty roomy.

'35

This ornate display merchandised the accessory right side wiper available for 1935 Chevrolet Master Deluxe models.

They Paid you $4,000,000 FOR CHEVROLET RADIOS DURING 1934

Use THE FREE TRIAL PLAN 7 OUT OF 10 BUY

1935 MASTER RUNNING BOARD ANTENNA

This radio display at a 1935 Chevrolet salesmen's meeting utilized real instrument panels to show the installation as it will be seen by the customer.

Here's a loaded 1935 Chevrolet Standard four-door Sedan. Among the visible accessories are wheel discs, dual trumpet horns, hood ornament, bumper guards, spotlight and clock mirror. Note fake scenery behind car.

Captain Bob Ward brings his 1935 Chevrolet Master Deluxe Coach in for a hard landing at a thrill show at the Detroit City Airport.

Here's a 1935 Chevrolet Standard Sedan Delivery. The single sidemount was standard on this vehicle.

A 1935 Chevrolet Standard four-door Sedan takes the stage at the dealer announcement show in Detroit's Masonic Temple.

A loaded 1935 Master Deluxe Coupe is seen on display in the Chevrolet tent at the University of Detroit's Mayfair Festival.

Some lucky person drove home from the Mayfair Festival in a new 1935 Chevrolet Master Deluxe Coach.

This long wheelbase 1935 Chevrolet Master Deluxe was a limited production model for export only. Although it carries a New York license plate, the vehicle was shot in Detroit on the roof of the General Motors Research Building.

A 1935 Chevrolet Station Wagon constructed on the commercial chassis was in the service of the U.S. Department of Interior's Soil Erosion Service.

Spotlights highlight a '35 Master Deluxe Sport Sedan during a studio shoot.

Close-up reveals the
Chevrolet bow-tie
emblem on the
hubcap.

1936: Hydraulic brakes and all-steel bodies

In 1936 the Standard and Master Deluxe series Chevrolets joined the ranks of vehicles using hydraulic brakes. The disappointing loss of sales superiority to Ford in 1935 undoubtedly caused a lot of internal refocusing on both product and promotion. The Standard which had sold fairly well in 1935 was looking dated. The traditionally more conservative buyer of Standards had been exposed to streamlined design for another year and Chevrolet guessed correctly that they would now be ready for a new look. These new 1936 Standards featured fresh new styling with the bodies derived from the previous Master deluxe. At 109 inches, the wheelbase was two inches greater than last year but still four inches less than that of the Master Deluxe. Integral trunks were now available on Standard models (and those models were in much greater demand than those with rear-mounted spares). Front doors were hinged at the front, rear hinging having proven unpopular. The new grilles were rounded and stood at a less dramatic angle. While not radical, these new Chevrolets, Standard and Master Deluxe, were completely in sync with the design expectations of the marketplace. The smaller 16-inch wheels of the Master Deluxes as well as their larger hubcaps, chromed headlamp shells, heavier bumpers and the longer wheelbase gave the prestige-minded buyer a better proportioned and more expensive looking car for an increase of about two to three additional dollars on the monthly car payment tempered by the expection of better resale value.

Both series now used the same engine giving the smaller, lighter Standards a little extra snap. A Cabriolet returned to the line this year in the Standard Series. Regrettably, the convertible body style was not offered in the better proportioned Master Deluxe line where it could have made for a beautiful vehicle. A solid front axle was again featured on Standards, available on Master Deluxes. During the year Fisher Body began phasing out composite construction (wood and steel) in favor of all-steel construction.

THIS IS THE
12 MILLIONTH
CHEVROLET
Built AUG. 5th.1936

Sales were brisk in 1934, '35 and '36, and Chevrolet hit a milestone in 1936 with the production of its 12-millionth car, this '36 Master Deluxe Sport Sedan. The Sport Sedan was the most expensive Chevy offered in 1936, listing for $685. It was also the heaviest at 3,135 pounds. Model year production for 1936 set a record at 931,012, and 140,073 of them were Master Sport Sedans.

The 1936 redesign theme for the nation's three most popular cars could be characterized as "more rounded, less pointed." Each got new front end styling with a more rounded grille replacing the pointed units of 1935. Ford also restyled its rear fenders to reduce the slight "kickup" of 1935 fenders. The wire wheels gave way to a new design which incorporated a large hubcap. In later years the 1936 Ford was to prove far more popular with hot-rodders and restorers who sometimes added 1936 sheet metal when restoring 1935 Fords. More recently the 1935 has acquired a following. The Plymouth facelift was probably at its best on touring sedans which took on a more contemporary look compared to the 1935 models. The most memorable feature of these Plymouths was the "fishbowl" instrument cluster, which housed all gauges and the speedometer under a huge glass lens in the middle of the dash. While both competitors were well accepted, the Chevrolet was obviously on target, especially with the new Standard. The Standard models accounted for 46 percent of production as Chevrolet again became the world's best-selling car.

The Standard Cabriolet was Chevrolet's only domestic open car in 1936. Like the other 1936 Standards, it featured a solid front axle and was built on the shorter 109-inch wheelbase.

This display shows some of the accessories available to personalize your new 1936 Chevrolet.

Wire wheels were available on the 1936 Chevrolet Master Deluxe Sport Sedan but weren't very common. This car is nicely optioned out.

This 1936 Chevrolet Master Deluxe Town Sedan shows off its accessory fender skirts.

The 1936 Chevrolet Sedan Delivery was an attractive little hauler on the Standard series 109-inch wheelbase.

The Knee-Action demonstration vehicle attracted an enthusiastic crowd at the Michigan State Fair in September 1936. A separate pair of Knee-Action units was stacked on top of the factory-installed units.

A load of new 1936 Master Deluxes is pulled by an unusual Chevrolet cab-over-engine tractor.

This 1936 Chevrolet
Master Deluxe wears
a 1936 California
dealer plate, dual
sidemounts and a
spotlight.

The chrome wheel discs are an unusual accessory on this very pretty 1936 Chevrolet Master Deluxe Town Sedan.

This unusual shot shows some of the 16 1936 Chevrolet Master Deluxe two-passenger Coupes with fifth-wheel trailers used by representatives of the Eclipse Lawn Mower Co.

A rare and attractive vehicle was this 1936 Chevrolet Master Deluxe Station Wagon. Although it was very tall, it managed to look rakish.

Checker Cab Co. of Detroit proudly displayed 25 new 1936 Chevrolet Master Deluxe four-door Sedans in front of the General Motors Building. It seems a bit odd, from this historical perspective, that they didn't select trunk models in the less expensive Standard series.

Not offered in the United States but still available in some export markets was this 1936 Chevrolet Standard Rumble Seat Roadster. Note missing instruments indicating that this was probably a prototype.

This 1936 Chevrolet Standard Phaeton was offered in selected export markets outside of the United States.

An extended wheelbase 1936 Chevrolet Master Deluxe: These were sold in certain European markets in sedan and convertible sedan configurations.

A modern
Chevrolet
dealership in
Detroit in 1936.

189

The 1936 Chevrolet Standard Coupe Delivery afforded the comfort and appearance of a passenger car with some of the cargo capacity of a light pickup.

1936 Chevrolets were part of the GM Building lobby Christmas display in December 1935. The Master Deluxe Sport Coupe is wearing a price tag of $590. Knee-Action was $20 extra.

This is the rear view of a 1936 Chevrolet Master Deluxe Sport Sedan. The taillight had moved to the fender and the trunk lid now used only one handle.

This front view of a 1936 Chevrolet Standard Cabriolet shows the interesting rear window shape and the top overlapping the windshield header. Notice the off-center mounting of the rear-view mirror.

36

The Chevrolet Retail Store in Detroit had this fully optioned 1936 Master Deluxe four-door Sedan rigged up with real neon signs. The one on the hood read "Knee-Action."

1937: 'Diamond Crown' styling

For 1937 Chevrolet returned to one wheelbase, 112.5 inches, for all passenger car models. The Master series replaced the previous year's Standard in the low end of the product line. The premium trim models were again found in the Master Deluxe series. The 1937 Master models were far more upscale visually then their Standard predecessors. The Master deluxe models all featured Knee-Action front suspension while Masters used the straight front axle with leaf springs. Fresh new "Diamond Crown" styling was shared by both series. Completely new and contemporary, the new Chevrolets managed to look more "mainstream" than the traditional competition. Plymouth, with all new styling and a solid steel roof, was all curves but clung to the old fashioned crank-out one-piece flat windshield. Ford went for the streamlined look but blunted the effect with high, stubby bodies.

In comparing the new Chevrolet Masters to the Master Deluxes, there were few external differences. Included were running board moldings on Master Deluxe models as well as contoured bumpers with slightly tapered ends while the Masters used a flat face bar. Master Deluxes got two taillights.

Inside, both vehicles were nicely trimmed but the Master Deluxes featured added touches like bright trim on the instrument panel, rubber clutch and brake pedal pads and carpet on the rear floor to replace the Standard's rubber mat. The one exception to this was the Master Cabriolet which combined the Master's solid front axle with the Master Deluxe's visual cues.

Five-window coupes were now the norm. Sport coupes (the rumble seat Master Deluxe) and the Cabriolet retained the rear mounted external spare tire which moved inside on the business coupe models. Sport Sedans and Town Sedans in both series sported integral trunks while the two and four-door sedans continued the rear mounted spare tire. Predictably, as in 1936, the security and convenience of the trunk models outweighed the lower prices of the regular sedans with the bulk of the sales going to those with the built-in trunk.

Ford and Plymouth both completely eliminated rear mounted spare tires and Ford no longer offered coupes with rumble seats. Ford's new styling was

Chevrolet's sweet Cabriolet was its only open model on the U.S. market for 1937. Just 1,724 were built. A rumble seat and rear-mounted spare were standard equipment. The car line was completely remodeled for '37.

clearly influenced by the Lincoln Zephyr but lacked the Zephyr's streamlined grace. The problem seemed to be that the body was just too thick resulting in a most un-Zephyrlike high, stubby look. Plymouth's new styling developed under the direction of well known body builder, Ray Dietrich, was conservative to a fault, retaining the old flat windshield and a rounded grille in an era of prow-shaped front ends. One piece steel roofs were now used on closed models of Chevrolet and the competition.

A 1937 Chevrolet Master Cabriolet is seen at a Detroit area horse show. Although a Master model with solid front axle, it carried Master Deluxe trim, including running board moldings.

A 1937 Chevrolet Sedan Delivery displays its new styling at an auto show. The unique rear bumper has a concave section to make loading and unloading easier.

This little sheet metal tray was a Chevrolet accessory. It is shown on a 1937 Master Deluxe dash. This view shows woodgrain garnish moldings and painted dash.

This detail shot of the rumble seat area of a 1937 Master Deluxe Sport Coupe also shows taillight and tire cover detail.

This high view of a 1937 Chevrolet Master Deluxe Sport Sedan shows the depth of the "speedline" originating in the fender catwalk and fading out in the front door.

This 1937 Master Deluxe has a banjo wheel, sunvisor glare shade, radio, and overhead speaker.

These fog lamps were available for 1937 Chevrolets. This view shows wheel stripes, fender welt detail and Master Deluxe bumper and guards.

A new owner receives the keys to his 1937 Master Town Sedan in front of the Angola Garage. A vintage bicycle can be seen at the rear.

Here's a rare one: A 1937 Chevrolet Master Deluxe four-door Sedan. Although the semi-fastback and rear-mounted spare had a rakish look, the buyers far preferred the practical trunk models.

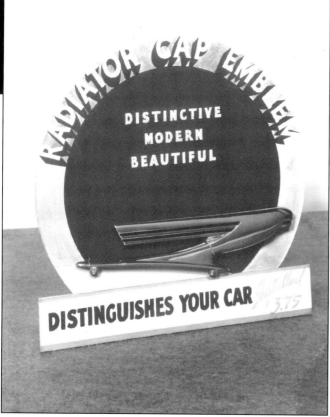

37

We call it a hood ornament but back in 1937 this was the accessory "radiator cap emblem," selling for $3.75 installed.

This display of 1937 Chevrolet genuine custom-built accessories includes a tantalizing array of goodies.

It would be hard to find a better angle from which to view the 1937 Chevrolet Master Cabriolet. Note the electric light illuminating the price card.

This is the Chevrolet display at the 1937 Detroit Auto Show. Horizontal lines and art deco themes were big at that time.

The 1937 Chevrolet Master Deluxe Coach in the background is one of only 7,250 built that year.

If you thought this was a scene from a 1950's Japanese sci-fi film, you're wrong. The girl is normal size. The 1937 Chevrolet Master Deluxe Sport Sedan is a very accurate model.

A 1937 Chevrolet Master Deluxe Business Coupe with wheel shields (skirts), fender lights, wheel discs and whitewalls was a handsome car.

The paint scheme on this 1937 Chevrolet Master Deluxe appears on other vehicles in the General Motors Media Archives. We believe that it was unique to dealer demonstrators. How about that motor scooter?

This cut-away of a 1937 Chevrolet Master Deluxe Knee-Action unit was displayed at the New York Auto Show.

The gentleman is pointing at an accessory fender guide which helped protect your 1937 Chevrolet's fenders when entering small garages.

Here's a whole room full of 1937 Chevrolet Master Deluxe show chassis intended for auto shows and dealer displays.

Competitive update: This is the main competitor, a 1937 Ford Deluxe fordor. Some buyers considered the new styling to be too radical.

Holding down the number three position in sales for 1937, Plymouth was more conservative in design than Chevrolet or Ford.

The 1937 Master Deluxe Sport Sedan is not actually in a chop shop. It was the subject of an engineering tear-down to measure component wear and improve the breed.

Here is the Chevrolet version of the long wheelbase 1937 taxi. Note that this vehicle does not have the integral trunk.

Looks like a long wheelbase 1937 Chevrolet doesn't it? Look closely at the hubcaps and hood ornament. This particular vehicle was badged as a GMC.

1938:
New grilles, trim; voltage regulator added

For 1938 Chevrolet continued the successful Master and Master Deluxe lines. The 1938 catalog explained the line this way: "These two series of cars, clearly similar in chassis and body design, are alike in essential qualities of appearance, safety and general dependability. They differ chiefly in front spring suspension, (Master Deluxe models have Knee-Action at no extra cost)." These new Chevrolets were very close relatives to the 1937 models they replaced. New grilles, hood trim, bumpers, door handles and deck lid

emblem pretty well summarized the exterior changes. The grille bars went from vertical to horizontal for a very different look.

Refinement is the perfect word to describe the changes in interior trim. The seat and door panel mohair was a lighter shade of tan with revised pleat design. The instrument panel trim changed as did the color of most interior sheet metal. The black steering wheel of 1937 became the beige wheel of 1938. The overall effect was that of a lighter, brighter interior. Trunk interiors in Town Sedan and Sport Sedan models were redesigned for 25 percent greater luggage capacity. The trunk shelf was removed and the spare tire placed upright. A telescoping trunk door support replaced the folding support of 1937. Tools were kept in a compartment under the floor extension.

Mechanical refinement started with a new clutch design with benefits in driving comfort, longer life and smoother operation. New engine features included improved water pump and fan assembly. Improved front end oil seal and more efficient carburetor choke. Electrical improvements included the addition of a voltage regulator and a completely redesigned starter. The hand brake now featured a release handle of the type that had been offered as an accessory on many cars of the period. New accessories for 1938 included illuminated vanity mirror, back-up light, windshield washer and rubber bladed fan.

In New Zealand, a right-hand-drive '38 Chevrolet Master Sedan was the tow vehicle of choice for an AC promotional trailer that advertised: "Have your plugs cleaned by the new AC method."

Chevrolet's facelift for 1938 was both simple and effective. The vehicles were fresh and more expensive looking, due entirely to rather inexpensive changes in ornamentation. Ford and, to a lesser extent, Plymouth made more extensive changes and were not as well received in the marketplace. The fastback bodies of the new Deluxe Fords were nicely streamlined but the grille design was unusual enough to turn off too many traditional buyers. The Standard Ford used the previous year's notchback body with a new front end and larger rear fenders. Shortly after introduction additional bright trim was added to the Standard to make it more acceptable but it just didn't have the visual appeal of the base Master Chevrolet. Plymouth managed to facelift its way into the public doghouse as well. Plymouth also was forced to make interim design changes, in this case the headlights were lowered to lessen the "bug-eye" look.

This shot clearly shows the frontal differences between 1938 (left) and 1937 (right) Chevrolet Master Deluxe Sport Sedans. Compare the bumpers, hoods and grilles.

This 1938 Chevrolet display chassis appeared at the Detroit Auto Show. The model is pointing to the cut-away muffler.

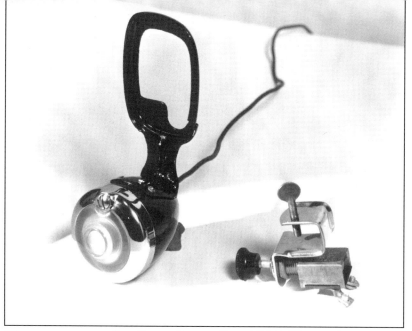

If you need a rare accessory trunk light for your 1938 Chevrolet, this is what you want.

The accessory back-up lamp for 1938 Chevrolets mounted between the taillight and the stand. The switch was manually activated.

The new premium radio for 1938 Chevrolets was this push-button unit. The radio, radio head and speaker were separate units.

The rear passenger compartment of a 1938 extended-wheelbase taxi is shown in this heavily retouched art. Everything was designed for easy clean-up.

This fan mounted behind the rear seat riser was part of a ventilation system referred to as "air conditioning" available for 1938 Chevrolets. Other elements included a small chrome scoop on the cowl side which fed outside air to the heater.

A well dressed 1938 Chevrolet Master Deluxe two-passenger Coupe attends a spring picnic.

The Chevrolet exhibit at the 1938 Detroit
Auto Show. The new grilles were used as
decorative elements on the component
display fixtures.

The new electrical system found on 1938 Chevrolets included a voltage regulator for the first time.

This auto show display shows the new clutch which was said to contribute to driving comfort.

The 1938 Chevrolet Master Deluxe instrument panel featured new trim in a horizontal motif. Beige and gray colors dominated.

This 1938 Chevrolet Master Deluxe Sport Sedan shows the new trunk emblem. Running board moldings were standard on Master Deluxe models. The circular spot beneath the emblem is a reflection of the photographic lighting.

This view of a 1938 Chevrolet Master Deluxe Sport Sedan reveals the Knee-Action unit peeking out behind the front tire.

This front view of a 1938 Chevrolet shows how the new hood extends over the top of the grille.

'38

The 1938 Chevrolet clutch and brake pedal pads displayed the bow-tie. Note that the radio speaker is center mounted and the radio is to the left. The new emergency brake release handle is shown.

The new Master Deluxe mohair fabric was a lighter shade of tan for 1938. The Sport Sedan is shown.

A 1938 Master Deluxe two-passenger Coupe. The fuel filler on this model was in the right quarter panel. Note the stone deflector on the rear bumper brackets.

A 1938 Master Town Sedan is in the showroom of Chevrolet's Detroit retail branch in the GM Building. The front bucket seats, used for the last time on this model, are visible. Master models did not receive the bright running board moldings.

The gentleman seated in the 1938 Chevrolet Cabriolet is Semon "Bunkie" Knudsen. Notice the wooden bulkhead in the rumble seat.

This cut-away shows the innards of the 1938 Master Deluxe Knee-Action unit, which contained a good sized coil spring.

The glimpse of a rear-mounted spare tire and the steps on the bumper and right rear fender tell us that the 1938 Chevrolet we are looking at is a Master Deluxe Sport Coupe. Check out those planters.

This 1938 Chevrolet Master Deluxe Town Sedan was photographed at the dealer preview at the General Motors Proving Ground at Milford, Mich.

This 1938 Chevrolet Master Cabriolet has at least six accessories, but it doesn't have the optional right windshield wiper.

The case mounted to the steering column of this 1938 Chevrolet Master Deluxe is dispensing a cigarette. At least six accessories are shown on a Sport Sedan.

Elegant showroom display spotlights the 1938 Chevrolet lineup.

The GM dealer in Formosa mounted a touring body on a commercial chassis to create this unique
1938 Chevrolet Touring car.

1939: Vacuum-shift debuts; no open model in the line

The year 1939 was one of beginnings and endings for Chevrolet. Again, two series, the Master Deluxe and the Master 85, were available. The new styling was closely linked to that of 1938. Above the belt line, styling was very similar, while below the belt line changes were pronounced. On Town Sedan and Sport Sedan models, the body sides swept back over the rear fenders to completely incorporate the integral trunk. The trunk-less sedans continued to feature the rear mounted spare tire with metal cover. This would be the last year for these models. Fenders were larger and

squared off, headlights moved down to rest on the cat walks and the center portion of the three-piece grille swept back dramatically. Taillights were mounted high on the body sides and the license plate was mounted high on the deck lid.

There were no open cars in Chevrolet's line for 1939. There was however, a lot to talk about in coupes, which bore little resemblance to their 1938 predecessors. Longer, more angular roofs allowed enough room for the folding "jump seats" of the new four-passenger coupe, which replaced the previous rumble seat equipped sport coupe. Business coupe models had a large interior luggage deck behind the front seat.

Inside, the new instrument panel was modern and attractive. Those buyers who elected to purchase the extra cost vacuum shift were rewarded with the new steering column mounted shift lever. The shift lever remained on the floor on non-vacuum shift vehicles in both series. To provide a truly clear floor, the new "trigger-control" emergency brake was located under the instrument panel to the left of the steering column.

Mechanically, the 1939 Chevrolet was the beneficiary of 10 years of advancement over the original Chevrolet Six of 1929. The engine was a much improved unit developing 85 horsepower. The simplified "tiptoe-matic clutch" was smoother and hydraulic brakes provided faster, more reliable stopping. Newly designed "perfected knee-action" was

A new look was achieved for 1939 with a sharply refined hood and fenders. Two series were produced in '39, the Master and Master Deluxe. The former was also known as the Master 85 Series. Model year output stood at 587,177, with the majority, 387,119, in the Master Deluxe line. No open models graced the '39 lineup. Another production milestone — the 15-millionth Chevrolet — was attained during the '39 model year.

more compact and more reliable than the original design of 1934. All steel bodies with steel roofs were far more durable, safer and quieter than their predecessors from the early part of the decade.

Competitively speaking, Chevrolet was facing better cars in 1939. Ford finally got hydraulic brakes and got its streamlining right, at least on the Deluxe models. Standard models looked like plainer versions of the 1938 Deluxe. Although modern in appearance, Fords were still perched on the same type of archaic

transverse springs that they employed at the beginning of the decade. Plymouth returned to independent front suspension, which patent problems had caused them to abandon in 1935. With new front ends, windshields and rear fenders, the Plymouths still used 1937-38 bodies. The public liked the new look of Chevrolet and the reward was yet another sales crown. In retrospect it is obvious that the early six-cylinder years definitely belonged to Chevrolet, which led the sales race in eight of those 11 years.

The arrows point to a camera inside the 1939 Chevrolet Master Deluxe Business Coupe and a speedometer mounted on the headlight. This combination recorded trucks traveling at excessive speeds. It was used by Eagle, Globe and Royal Indemnity Companies.

A 1939 Chevrolet Master Deluxe Business Coupe shows its new, more squared off roof line.

The 1939 Master 85 Town Sedan was the first of the Chevrolet low-line two-doors to feature a bench seat replacing the familiar buckets.

This angle shows the dramatic sweep of the grille and the catwalk-mounted headlights of a 1939 Chevrolet Master Deluxe Business Coupe.

Chevrolet executives gather around the 500,000th 1939 Chevrolet. Note the accessory chrome grilles on the fender vents.

According to the press release that accompanied this shot, the folks around the 1939 Chevrolet Master Deluxe Town Sedan are members of the Flint Mich. Polar Bear Club. Brrrrrr.

In April of 1939 Detroit's auto dealers displayed new 1939 cars and their 1929 counterparts on elegant Washington Boulevard. This was one of the 1939 Chevrolets. Notice that the 1929 Chevrolet is actually a 1928 model.

This streamlined 1939 Ford Deluxe was the first Ford to get hydraulic brakes. This one is wearing whitewalls, fog lights and a roof mounted radio antenna.

'39

Muncey Chevrolet opened a new showroom in July 1939. The showroom stock included a 1939 Master Deluxe Coupe and a Master 85 Town Sedan. Bins of accessories shared the display area.

This is the exterior of Muncey Chevrolet's new facility in 1939. It was at the corner of Greenlawn and W. McNichols Road in Northwest Detroit.

A very well accessorized 1939 Chevrolet Master Deluxe Town Sedan is on the rack at Marsh-Grosfield Chevrolet in Henry Ford's hometown, Dearborn, Mich. The Harley was towed behind customer's vehicles being brought in for service.

This 1939 Chevrolet Master Deluxe Sport Sedan has several nice options. Note the wheel discs. It was on display at the 1939 New York World's Fair.

A 1939 Master Deluxe Sport Sedan. The right side windshield wiper was still an extra cost item and this car doesn't have one. A Willys is in the background.

The 1939 Chevrolet Business Coupe had plenty of trunk space as demonstrated by this Master Deluxe. Unlike sedans, the coupe carried its spare tire under a shelf.

On vacuum-shift models of 1939 Chevrolets the gear shift lever was mounted on the steering column and featured a flat knob.

The "stretch" area in this 1939 export model Chevrolet 7-passenger Sedan is all in the rear door.

The large luggage compartment of a 1939 Chevrolet Master 85 Town Sedan is shown here. The spare tire stood upright at the rear.

This profile shot makes it easy to see that this 1939 Chevrolet Master Deluxe Sport Sedan shared little with its 1938 counterpart, although they weren't radically different in appearance.

These 1939 Chevrolet Master Deluxes are being examined by Chevrolet's Collegiate Crew consisting of Harvard, Yale and Princeton students. These students would become hosts at the Chevrolet exhibit at the New York World's Fair after extensive product training.

Certainly the most valuable and arguably the best looking of all 1939 Chevrolets, the Master Deluxe Station Wagon could carry eight passengers and their luggage.

This neat little gadget was offered by Chevrolet in 1939. The hose connection allowed owners to check the spare tire inflation without opening and unloading the trunk.

(At right) Northwest Chevrolet was on Detroit's Grand River Ave. Its new Art Deco showroom featured recessed lighting and a 1939 Master Deluxe Business Coupe.

Look closely at this display of Chevrolet authorized accessories for 1939 and you will find some real bargains.